Garfield
Going Places

JIM DAVIS

D1368991

RR
RAVETTE BOOKS

First published by Ravette Books Limited 1990
Reprinted 1990, 1991, 1992

Printed and bound in Great Britain
for Ravette Books Limited,
3 Glenside Estate, Star Road, Partridge Green,
Horsham, West Sussex RH13 8RA
An Egmont Company
by Cox & Wyman Ltd, Reading

ISBN 1 85304 242 0

© 1988 United Feature Syndicate, Inc.

© 1988 United Feature Syndicate, Inc.

JIM DAVIS 9-14

IN CASE YOU'RE INTERESTED, WATCHES DON'T FLOAT

HE ACTUALLY MOVED

ONE SIDE WAS GETTING FLAT

JIM DAVIS 9-26

© 1988 United Feature Syndicate, Inc.

YOU MIGHT BE INTERESTED TO KNOW WHILE *YOU* WERE ASLEEP, I CAUGHT A MOUSE

GOOD BOY

JIM DAVIS

9-29

© 1988 United Feature Syndicate, Inc.

WHIP

A LITTLE SENSITIVE ABOUT OUR WEIGHT, ARE WE?

MY WEIGHT, MY BUSINESS

JIM DAVIS

10-11

10-24

JIM DAVIS   10-26

© 1988 United Feature Syndicate, Inc.

© 1988 United Feature Syndicate, Inc.

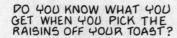

© 1988 United Feature Syndicate, Inc.

© 1988 United Feature Syndicate, Inc.

© 1988 United Feature Syndicate, Inc.

© 1988 United Feature Syndicate, Inc.

DARN THING'S DEFECTIVE

JIM DAVIS

12-23

THIS YEAR, I RESOLVE TO BE GENTLER WITH ODIE!

© 1988 United Feature Syndicate, Inc.

PUSH

JIM DAVIS 12-30

© 1988 United Feature Syndicate, Inc.

GARFIELD, I KNOW DIETING IS TOUGH FOR YOU

1-7-89

BUT, YOU'VE REALLY SUNK TO THE DEPTHS THIS TIME!

HEY! I'M SURE I'M NOT THE FIRST DIETER TO LICK THE PAGES OF HIS CANDY WRAPPER COLLECTION

JIM DAVIS

© 1989 United Feature Syndicate, Inc.

YES, EVEN YOUR TOE IS OVERWEIGHT

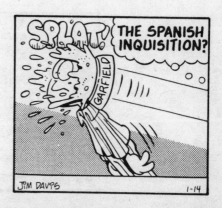

OTHER GARFIELD BOOKS IN THIS SERIES

COLOUR TV SPECIALS

Here Comes Garfield	£2.95
Garfield On The Town	£2.95
Garfield In The Rough	£2.95
Garfield In Disguise	£2.95
Garfield In Paradise	£2.95
Garfield Goes To Hollywood	£2.95
A Garfield Christmas	£2.95
Garfield's Thanksgiving	£2.95
Garfield's Feline Fantasies	£2.95
Garfield Gets A Life	£2.95
Garfield A Weekend Away	£4.95
Garfield Book Of Cat Names	£2.50
Garfield Best Ever	£4.95
Garfield Selection	£5.95
Garfield How To Party	£3.95
Garfield The Easter Bunny?	£3.95
Garfield His 9 Lives	£5.95
The Garfield Diet Book	£4.95
Garfield Exercise Book	£4.95
Garfield Book Of Love	£5.95

All these books are available at your local bookshop or newsagent, or can be ordered direct from the publisher. Just tick the titles you require and fill in the form below. Prices and availability subject to change without notice.

Ravette Books Limited, 3 Glenside Estate, Star Road, Partridge Green, Horsham, West Sussex RH13 8RA

Please send a cheque or postal order and allow the following for postage and packing. UK: Pocket-books – 45p for one book, 20p for a second book and 15p for each additional book. Landscape Series – 50p for one book plus 30p for each additional book. TV Specials and Cat Names – 45p for one book plus 30p for each additional book. Other titles – 85p for one book plus 50p for each additional book ordered.

Name ....

Address ....

....